ISBN 978-1-998317-73-8

Cover design by Charlotte Chang.

First Edition: February, 2025

Jirafa
Giraffe

Mapache
Raccoon

Ardilla
Squirrel

Jabalí
Wild Boar

Caballo
Horse

Camello
Camel

Castor
Beaver

Oso pardo
Brown Bear

Cabra
Goat

Oso polar
Polar Bear

Alpaca
Alpaca

Zorro ártico
Arctic Fox

Cisne
Swan

Gata/Gato
Cat

Armiño
Ermine

Conejo/Coneja
Rabbit

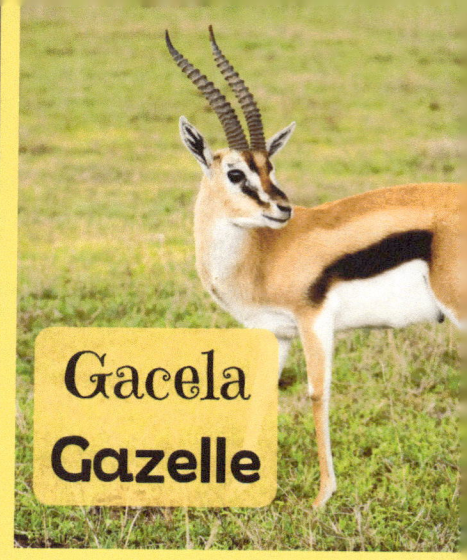

Gacela
Gazelle

León
Lion

Mono dorado
Golden Monkey

Canguro
Kangaroo

Perro golden retriever
Golden retriever dog

Oropéndola amarilla
Yellow oriole

Zorro fénec
Fennec Fox

Dingo
Dingo

Canario
Canary

Mariposa azufrada
Sulphur butterfly

Cuervo
Crow

Pantera
Panther

Oso negro
Black Bear

Chimpancé
Chimpanzee

Zorro plateado
Silver Fox

Diablo de Tasmania
Tasmanian Devil

Gibón
Gibbon

Drongo negro
Black Drongo

Panda rojo
Red Panda

Zorro rojo
Red Fox

Canguro rojo
Red Kangaroo

Orangután
Orangutan

Guacamayo escarlata
Scarlet Macaw

Flamenco
Flamingo

Mandril
Mandrill

Mosquero cardenal
Vermilion Flycatcher

Mantis religiosa
Praying Mantis

Paloma esmeralda
Emerald dove

Periquito
Parakeet

Barbudo oliváceo
Green barbet

Cebra
Zebra

Mofeta
Skunk

Pingüino
Penguin

Panda
Panda

Tejón
Badger

Búho nival
Snowy Owl

Tapir malayo
Malayan Tapir

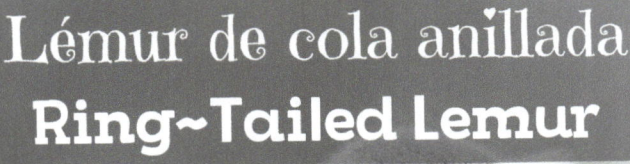

Lémur de cola anillada
Ring~Tailed Lemur

Leopardo
Leopard

Okapi
Okapi

Hiena manchada
Spotted Hyena

Ocelote
Ocelot

Caballo appaloosa
Appaloosa horse

Perro salvaje africano
African Wild Dog

Ciervo moteado
Spotted deer

Tigre
Tiger

Martín pescador
Kingfisher

Pavo real
Peacock

Arrendajo azul
Blue Jay

Mariposa morpho azul
Blue Morpho Butterfly

Guacamayo jacinto
Hyacinth macaw

Rana punta de flecha azul
Blue Poison Dart Frog

Azulillo índigo
Indigo bunting

Azulejo
Bluebird

Nutria
Otter

Rinoceronte
Rhinoceros

Hipopótamo
Hippopotamus

Topo
Mole

Elefante
Elephant

Uómbat
Wombat

Lobo gris
Gray Wolf

Burro
Donkey

Chinchilla
Chinchilla

Loro
Parrot

Pato mandarín
Mandarin Duck

Tucán
Toucan

Lori arcoíris
Rainbow Lorikeet

Mariposa monarca
Monarch Butterfly

Faisán dorado
Golden Pheasant

Rana arlequín
Harlequin Tree Frog

Tití león dorado
Golden Lion Tamarin

Mariquita
Ladybug

Quetzal
Quetzal

Hámster
Hamster

Carpincho
Capybara

Erizo
Hedgehog

Suricata
Meerkat

Perezoso
Sloth

Agutí
Agouti

Bisonte
Bison

www.ingramcontent.com/pod-product-compliance
Lightning Source LLC
Chambersburg PA
CBHW041450120626
46547CB00002B/406